The Ultimate Wood Pellet Grill And Smoker Cookbook

A Simplified Guide To Prepare The Greatest Grill You Have Ever Had And Become The Most Renowned Bbq Pitmasters In Your Family

LIAM JONES

Table of Contents

BREAKFAST RECIPES 9

    1.   Bacon Chocolate Chip Cookies 10

    2.   Chocolate Chip Cookies... 12

    3.   Apple Cobbler 14

    4.   Caramel Bananas 16

FISH AND SEAFOOD RECIPES 19

    5.   Fish Stew 20

    6.   Whole Vermillion Snapper... 22

    7.   Smoked Sea Bass 23

CHICKEN AND TURKEY RECIPES... 26

    49.   Teriyaki Turkey.. 27

    50.   Cheesy Turkey Burger 29

    51.   Turkey Sandwich.. 31

    52.   Smoked Turkey 32

    53.   Tasty Chicken Satay... 33

    54.   Easy Grilled Chicken... 35

    55.   Chicken with Lemon Yogurt.................................... 37

BEEF RECIPES... 40

    56.   Garlic, Lemon, and Goat Cheese Mashed Potatoes 41

57.   Wood pellet Prime Rib Roast..................................... 43

58.   Italian Beef Sandwich 45

LAMB RECIPES.. 48

18.   Lamb Wraps... 48

19.   Morrocan Kebabs 50

20.   Steamed Lamb Shank 52

21.   Braised Lamb Tacos 53

PORK RECIPES.. 56

22.   Simple Wood Pellet Smoked Pork Ribs 56

23.   Roasted Pork with Balsamic Strawberry Sauce.................. 58

24.   Cocoa Crusted Pork Tenderloin.............................. 60

25.   Wood Pellet Grilled Bacon..................................... 62

APPETIZERS AND SIDES.. 64

26.   Cheesy Sausage Balls... 64

27.   Corn and Crab Cakes.. 66

28.   Brisket Baked Beans 68

29.   Twice-Baked Spaghetti Squash 70

30.   Bacon-Wrapped Asparagus 73

VEGETARIAN RECIPES 76

31.   Smoked Cauliflower.. 77

32. Smoked Cheesy Potatoes Casserole 79

33. Vegetarian Hot Dogs with Spicy Jalapeño Relish 80

34. Grilled Citrus Shrimp Lettuce Cups 82

35. Broccoli and Cheddar Stuffed Potatoes 84

GAME AND ORIGINAL RECIPES 87

36. Aromatic Smoked Duck Breast 87

37. Smoked Quails 89

38. Smoked Venison 91

39. Smoked Rabbit 93

SNACKS 96

40. Spiced Nuts 96

BREAKFAST RECIPES

1. *Bacon Chocolate Chip Cookies*

Preparation Time: 30 minutes

Cooking Time: 30 minutes

Servings: 6

Ingredients:

- 8 slices cooked and crumbled bacon
- 2 ½ teaspoon apple cider vinegar
- 1 teaspoon vanilla
- 2 cup semisweet chocolate chips
- 2 room temp eggs
- 1 ½ teaspoon baking soda
- 1 cup granulated sugar
- ½ teaspoon salt
- 2 ¾ cup all-purpose flour
- 1 cup light brown sugar
- 1 ½ stick softened butter

Directions:

1. Mix salt, baking soda, and flour.
2. Cream the sugar and the butter together. Lower the speed. Add in the eggs, vinegar, and vanilla.
3. Put it on low fire, slowly add in the flour mixture, bacon pieces, and chocolate chips.

4. Add Preferred Wood Pellet pellets to your smoker and follow your cooker's startup procedure. Preheat your smoker, with your lid closed, until it reaches 375.

5. Put parchment paper on a baking sheet you are using and drop a teaspoonful of cookie batter on the baking sheet. Let them cook on the grill, covered, for approximately 12 minutes or until they are browned.

Nutrition: Calories: 167 Carbs: 21g Fat: 9g Protein: 2g

2. *Chocolate Chip Cookies*

Preparation Time: 30 minutes

Cooking Time: 30 minutes

Servings: 8

Ingredients:

- 1 ½ cup chopped walnuts
- 1 teaspoon vanilla
- 2 cup chocolate chips
- 1 teaspoon baking soda
- 2 ½ cup plain flour
- ½ teaspoon salt
- 1 ½ stick softened butter
- 2 eggs
- 1 cup brown sugar
- ½ cup sugar

Directions:

1. Add Preferred Wood Pellet pellets to your smoker and follow your cooker's startup procedure. Preheat your smoker, with your lid closed, until it reaches 350.
2. Mix the baking soda, salt, and flour.
3. Cream the brown sugar, sugar, and butter. Mix in the vanilla and eggs until it comes together.

4. Slowly add in the flour while continuing to beat. Once all flour has been incorporated, add in the chocolate chips and walnuts. Using a spoon, fold into batter.

5. Place an aluminum foil onto the grill. In an aluminum foil, drop a spoonful of dough and bake for 17 minutes.

Nutrition: Calories: 150 Carbs: 18g Fat: 5g Protein: 10g

3. *Apple Cobbler*

Preparation Time: 30 minutes

Cooking Time: 1 hour 50 minutes

Servings: 8

Ingredients:

- 8 Granny Smith apples
- 1 cup sugar
- 1 stick melted butter
- 1 teaspoon cinnamon
- Pinch salt
- ½ cup brown sugar
- 2 eggs
- 2 teaspoons baking powder
- 2 cup plain flour
- 1 ½ cup sugar

Directions:

1. Peel and quarter apples, place into a bowl. Add in the cinnamon and one c. sugar. Stir well to coat and let it set for one hour.

2. Add Preferred Wood Pellet pellets to your smoker and follow your cooker's startup procedure. Preheat your smoker, with your lid closed, until it reaches 350.

3. In a large bowl add the salt, baking powder, eggs, brown sugar, sugar, and flour. Mix until it forms crumbles.

4. Place apples into a Dutch oven. Add the crumble mixture on top and drizzle with melted butter.

5. Place on the grill and cook for 50 minutes.

Nutrition: Calories: 152 Carbs: 26g Fat: 5g Protein: 1g

4. _Caramel Bananas_

Preparation Time: 15 minutes.

Cooking Time: 15 minutes.

Servings: 4

Ingredients:

- 1/3 cup chopped pecans
- ½ cup sweetened condensed milk
- 4 slightly green bananas
- ½ cup brown sugar
- 2 tablespoons corn syrup
- ½ cup butter

Directions:

1. Add pellet to your smoker and follow your cooker's startup procedure. Preheat your smoker, with the lid closed, until it reaches 350.

2. Place the milk, corn syrup, butter, and brown sugar into a heavy saucepan and bring to boil. For five minutes simmer the mixture in low heat. Stir frequently.

3. Place the bananas with their peels on, on the grill, and let them grill for five minutes. Flip and cook for five minutes more. Peels will be dark and might split.

4. Place on serving platter. Cut the ends off the bananas and split peel down the middle. Take the peel off the bananas and spoon caramel on top. Sprinkle with pecans.

Nutrition: Calories: 152 Carbs: 36g Fat: 1g Protein: 1g

FISH AND SEAFOOD RECIPES

5. *Fish Stew*

Preparation Time: 20 minutes

Cooking Time: 25 minutes

Servings: 8

Pellet: Oak

Ingredients:

- 1 jar (28oz.) Crushed Tomatoes
- 2 oz. of Tomato paste
- ¼ cup of White wine
- ¼ cup of Chicken Stock
- 2 tbsp. Butter
- 2 Garlic cloves, minced
- ¼ Onion, diced
- ½ lb. Shrimp divined and cleaned
- ½ lb. of Clams
- ½ lb. of Halibut
- Parsley
- Bread

Directions:

1. Preheat the grill to 300°F with a closed lid.
2. Place a Dutch oven over medium heat and melt the butter.

3. Sauté the onion for 4 - 7 minutes. Add the garlic—cook one more minute.

4. Add the tomato paste. Cook until the color becomes rust red. Pour the stock and wine. Cook 10 minutes. Add the tomatoes, simmer.

5. Chop the halibut, and together with the other seafood, add in the Dutch oven. Place it on the grill and cover it with a lid.

6. Let it cook for 20 minutes.

7. Season with black pepper and salt and set aside.

8. Top with chopped parsley and serve with bread. Enjoy!

Nutrition: Amount per 214 g = 1 serving(s) Calories: 188 Protein: 25g Carbs: 7g Fat: 12g

6. *Whole Vermillion Snapper*

Preparation Time: 15 minutes

Cooking Time: 25 minutes

Servings: 6

Pellet: Alder

Ingredients:

- 2 Rosemary springs
- 4 Garlic cloves, chopped (peeled)
- 1 Lemon, thinly sliced
- Black pepper
- Sea Salt
- 1 Vermillion Snapper, gutted and scaled

Directions:

1. Preheat the grill to high with a closed lid.
2. Stuff the fish with garlic. Sprinkle with rosemary, black pepper, sea salt, and stuff with lemon slices.
3. Grill for 25 minutes.
4. Serve and enjoy!

Nutrition: Amount per 115 g = 1 serving(s) Calories: 240 Protein: 43g Carbs: 0g Fat: 3g

7. *Smoked Sea Bass*

Preparation Time: 10 minutes

Cooking Time: 40 minutes

Servings: 4

Pellet: Apple

Ingredients:

Marinade:

- 1 tsp. Blackened Saskatchewan
- 1 tbsp. Thyme, fresh
- 1 tbsp. Oregano, fresh
- 8 cloves of Garlic, crushed
- 1 lemon, the juice
- ¼ cup oil

Sea Bass:

- 4 Sea bass fillets, skin off
- Chicken Rub Seasoning
- Seafood Seasoning (like Old Bay)
- 8 tbsp. Gold Butter

For garnish:

- Thyme
- Lemon

Directions:

1. Make the marinade: In a Ziploc bag, combine the ingredients and mix. Add the fillets and marinate for 30 min in the fridge. Turn once.

2. Preheat the grill to 325°F with a closed lid.

3. In a dish for baking, add the butter. Remove the fish from the marinade and pour it into the baking dish. Season the fish with chicken and seafood rub. Place it in the baking dish and on the grill. Cook 30 minutes. Baste 1 - 2 times.

4. Remove from the grill when the internal temperature is 160°F.

5. Garnish with lemon slices and thyme. Enjoy!

Nutrition: Amount per 145 g = 1 serving(s) Calories: 220 Protein: 32g Carbs: 1g Fat: 8g

8. *Teriyaki Turkey*

Preparation Time: 30 Minutes

Cooking Time: 4 Hours

Servings: 10

Ingredients:

Glaze

- 1/4 cup melted butter
- 1/2 cup apple cider
- 2 cloves garlic, minced
- 1/2 teaspoon ground ginger
- 2 tablespoons soy sauce
- 2 tablespoons honey

Turkey

- 2 tablespoons chicken seasoning
- 1 whole turkey

Thickener

- 1 tablespoon cold water
- 1 teaspoon cornstarch

Directions:

1. Add the glaze ingredients to a pan over medium heat.

2. Bring to a boil and then simmer for 5 minutes.

3. Reserve 5 tablespoons of the mixture.

4. Add the remaining to a marinade injection.

5. Place the turkey in a baking pan.

6. Season with the chicken seasoning.

7. Turn on the wood pellet grill.

8. Set it to 300 degrees F.

9. Add the turkey to the grill.

10. Cook for 3 hours.

11. Add the thickener to the reserved mixture.

12. Brush the turkey with this sauce.

13. Cook for another 1 hour.

Nutrition: Calories 935 Total fat 53g Saturated fat 15g Protein 107g Sodium 320mg

9. *Cheesy Turkey Burger*

Preparation Time: 20 Minutes

Cooking Time: 3 Hours

Servings: 8

Ingredients:

- 3 lb. ground turkey
- Burger seasoning
- 7 oz. brie cheese, sliced into cubes
- 8 burger buns, sliced
- Blueberry jam
- 2 roasted bell peppers, sliced

Directions:

1. Season the turkey with the burger seasoning.
2. Mix well.
3. Form 8 patties from the mixture.
4. Press cheese into the patties.
5. Cover the top with more turkey.
6. Preheat your wood pellet grill to 350 degrees F.
7. Cook the turkey burgers for 30 to 40 minutes per side.
8. Spread the burger buns with blueberry jam.
9. Add the turkey burger on top.
10. Top with the bell peppers.

Nutrition: Calories 935 Total fat 53g Saturated fat 15g Protein 107g Sodium 320mg

10. Turkey Sandwich

Preparation Time: 5 Minutes

Cooking Time: 25 Minutes

Servings: 4

Ingredients:

- 8 bread slices
- 1 cup gravy
- 2 cups turkey, cooked and shredded

Directions:

1. Set your wood pellet grill to smoke.
2. Preheat it to 400 degrees F.
3. Place a grill mat on top of the grates.
4. Add the turkey on top of the mat.
5. Cook for 10 minutes.
6. Toast the bread in the flame broiler.
7. Top the bread with the gravy and shredded turkey.

Nutrition: Calories 935 Total fat 53g Saturated fat 15g Protein 107g Sodium 320mg

11. *Smoked Turkey*

Preparation Time: 30 Minutes

Cooking Time: 6 Hours and 30 Minutes

Servings: 8

Ingredients:

- 1 cup butter
- 1/2 cup maple syrup
- 2 tablespoons chicken seasoning
- 1 whole turkey

Directions:

1. Add the butter to a pan over low heat.
2. Stir in the maple syrup.
3. Simmer for 5 minutes, stirring.
4. Turn off the stove and let cool.
5. Add to a marinade injection.
6. Inject into the turkey.
7. Add the turkey to the wood pellet grill.
8. Set it smoke.
9. Smoke at 275 degrees F for 6 hours.

Nutrition: Calories 935 Total fat 53g Saturated fat 15g Protein 107g Sodium 320mg

12. Tasty Chicken Satay

Preparation Time: 25 Minutes

Cooking Time: 20 Minutes

Servings: 20

Ingredients:

- Twenty wooden skewers
- six reaches boneless, skinless chicken breasts, cut lengthwise into strips
- six tablespoons soy sauce
- six tablespoons tomato sauce
- two tablespoons peanut oil
- four cloves garlic, minced
- half teaspoon ground black pepper
- half teaspoon ground cumin

Peanut Sauce:

- one tablespoon peanut oil
- ¼ onion, finely chopped
- one clove garlic, minced
- eight tablespoons peanut butter
- three tablespoons white sugar
- two tablespoons soy sauce
- one cup of water

- Half lemon, juiced

Directions:

1. Place wooden skewers in the deep dish and wrap with water and allow soaking for twenty minutes.
2. Take bowls add chicken strips and merge tomato sauce, peanut oil, soy sauce, cumin, pepper, and garlic in the little bowl and merge to combine.
3. Pour chicken strips and merge chicken is coated well on each side.
4. Marinate for fifteen minutes.
5. Now, form peanut sauce. After this, add one tablespoon of oil in the warm skillet over the intermediate to high heat. Add garlic and onion and cook it well. Stir until the onion gets translucent and soft for four minutes.
6. Now, add soy sauce, butter, water, and sugar and merge well. Cook well until the sauce gets thicken slowly for five minutes. Add in the juice of a lemon and eliminate it from the flame.
7. After this, preheat a grill for elevated heat and then lightly oil the grate. Thread every chicken strip on the skewer.
8. Keep skewers on the preheated grill and fry for ten minutes and flipping through cooking. Serve the satay skewers instantly with peanut sauce.

Nutrition: Calories 935 Total fat 53g Saturated fat 15g Protein 107g Sodium 320mg

13. *Easy Grilled Chicken*

Preparation Time: 10 Minutes

Cooking Time: 35 Minutes

Servings: 12

Ingredients:

- Two cups white distilled vinegar
- Two cups of water
- Two sticks butter
- Four tablespoons Worcestershire sauce
- Two teaspoons minced garlic
- Two bone-in chicken breasts
- Four medium chicken leg quarters
- Four tablespoons garlic salt

Two **Directions**:

- tablespoons ground black pepper
- One tablespoon white sugar

1. Merge Worcestershire sauce, water, vinegar, butter, minced garlic, garlic salt, sugar in the pot and boil it. Eliminate from the flame and allow the marinade to cool at room temperature for approximate half-hour.

2. Add chicken in the plastic bag, pour marinade over the chicken, seal it, and then preserve it for eight to the whole night.

3. After, preheat the grill for intermediate to elevate heat lightly oil the grate.

4. Move chicken pieces to the grill and stir it well, remove the marinade

5. Grill chicken until it gets pink in the middle for thirty to forty-five minutes. The thermometer is inserted in the bone temperature reaches 165F.

Nutrition: Calories 935 Total fat 53g Saturated fat 15g Protein 107g Sodium 320mg

14. Chicken with Lemon Yogurt

Preparation Time: 15 Minutes

Cooking Time: 35 Minutes

Servings: 6

Ingredients:

- Half cup plain low-fat Greek yogurt
- Half lemon, juiced
- One tablespoon lemon zest
- One teaspoon herb de Provence
- One teaspoon salt
- One teaspoon ground black pepper
- one whole chicken, cut into eight pieces
- One tablespoon olive oil
- Four cloves garlic,
- One tablespoon paprika
- Half cup plain low-fat Greek yogurt
- One tablespoon lemon juice
- One teaspoon harissa
- One pinch salt

Directions:

1. First, whisk half juice from olive oil, one teaspoon salt, half cup yogurt, lemon zest, paprika, herbs de Provence, garlic,

juice of the half lemon, and black pepper in the bowl. Pour into the plastic bag and then add chicken. Now, coat with marinade and squeeze out the extra air, close the bag. Preserve in the freezer for three hours.

2. Preheat the grill for intermediate to high heat and then lightly oil the grate.

3. Mix one tablespoon lemon juice, harissa, half cup yogurt in the little bowl and keep aside.

4. Eliminate the chicken from the plastic bag and move to the baking sheet lined or plate with paper towels. Now, pat chicken parts dry with more paper towels and then season with a pinch of salt.

5. Now, grill chicken on the preheated grill for at least two minutes, turn every piece, and transfer to indirect heat.

6. Grill and turning frequently by using lid until it gets browned and meat gets no longer pink in the middle for thirty to thirty-five minutes.

7. Taking a thermometer and insert it in the thickest part of the thigh near the bone. The thermometer should read 165 degrees.

8. Now, serve the chicken with a mixture of yogurt harissa on the side.

Nutrition: Calories 935 Total fat 53g Saturated fat 15g Protein 107g Sodium 320mg

15. *Garlic, Lemon, and Goat Cheese Mashed Potatoes*

Preparation Time: 1 hour and 15 minutes

Cooking Time: 20 minutes

Servings: 6-8 **Servings**

Ingredients:

- 1 head garlic
- 1 tsp olive oil
- 3 lbs. Yukon gold potatoes, peeled and chopped
- ¾ cup crumbled goat's cheese
- ¼ cup melted butter, plus more for drizzling
- ¾ cup heavy whipped cream
- Sea salt & freshly cracked black pepper
- 2 tsp fresh chives, finely diced

Directions:

1. When ready to cook, set the Smoke Temperature to 350 F and preheat, lid closed, for 10 to 15 minutes.

2. Using a sharp knife, slice about 1/8" off the top of the garlic head (leaving the root intact), exposing the individual garlic cloves. Drizzle the olive oil on top of the exposed garlic and season with a pinch of salt and pepper. Tightly wrap the bulb in aluminum foil and roast on the Wood pellet for 30 - 35

minutes, until the cloves are soft. Remove the garlic cloves and mash into a paste with a fork.

3. Meanwhile, bring a large stockpot of salted water to a boil over medium-high heat. Add the potatoes and cook for 15 - 20 minutes, or until softened and hashable. Drain and return to the pot, stirring until dry. Remove from Preferred Wood Pellet and stir in the cream, goat cheese, lemon zest, garlic mash, and ¼ cup of butter. Mash until smooth, and if you like it, whip that business up with a whisk. Season with salt and pepper to taste. Garnish with extra chives and a generous drizzle of melted butter. Enjoy!

Nutrition: Calories: 282kcal Carbohydrates: 24g | Protein: 8g | Fat: 17g | Saturated Fat: 10g Cholesterol: 45mg | Sodium: 391mg Potassium: 809mg | Fiber: 4g Vitamin A: 480IU Vitamin C: 21.5mg Calcium: 79mg Iron: 6.4mg

16. Wood pellet Prime Rib Roast

Preparation Time: 20 minutes

Cooking Time: 3 hours

Servings: 10

Ingredients:

- 1 (5-7 bones) prime rib roast
- Wood pellet prime rib rub, as needed

Directions:

1. Coat the roast evenly with the Wood pellet Prime Rib Rub and wrap in plastic wrap. Let sit in the refrigerator for 24 hours.
2. When ready to cook, set the Smoke Temperature too High and preheat, lid closed for 15 minutes.
3. Place the prime rib fat side up, directly on the grill grate, and cook for 30 minutes. Starting at a higher heat will help to develop a crispy, rendered crust.
4. After 30 minutes, reduce the grill Smoke Temperature to 325 F.
5. Close lid and roast at 325 F for 3-4 hours or until cooked to desired internal Smoke Temperature, 120 F for rare, 130 F for medium-rare, 140 F for medium, and 150 F for well done.
6. Remove from grill and let rest 15 minutes before carving. Enjoy!

Nutrition: Calories: 946kcal | Protein: 43g | Fat: 84g | Saturated Fat: 35g Cholesterol: 192mg | Sodium: 141mg Potassium: 701mg Calcium: 24mg   Iron: 4.5mg

17. *Italian Beef Sandwich*

Preparation Time: 5 minutes

Cooking Time: 4 hours and 15 minutes

Servings: 8 **Servings**

Ingredients:

- 1 Qty. (4 Lb.) Lean, Boneless Beef Roast (Sirloin or Top Round)
- Salt
- Pepper
- 4 cloves garlic, thinly sliced
- Wood pellet prime rib rub
- 6 cups beef broth
- 8 hoagie-style buns (for sandwiches)
- 6 slices Swiss cheese
- 1 cup bottled Giardiniera (Italian pickled vegetables; optional), chopped

Directions:

1. When ready to cook, set the Smoke Temperature to 450°F and preheat, lid closed for 15 minutes.
2. Season the roast liberally with salt, pepper, and Wood pellet prime rib rub. Using a paring knife, make 10-15 slits in the roast every 1" or so. Insert a garlic clove into each slit.

3. Place the roast directly on the grill grate and cook for about 1 hour flipping halfway through until browned well.

4. Remove the roast from the grill and transfer to a deep Dutch oven. Pour the beef broth over the roast. Cover tightly with foil and place back on the grill. Reduce the grill Smoke Temperature to 300°F and cook the roast for 3-4 hours or until it is fork-tender.

5. While the roast cooks, chop the giardiniera into small pieces.

6. Remove the Dutch oven from the grill and shred removing any large bits of fat or connective tissue. Transfer the meat back to the Dutch oven and stir to combine with the juices.

7. Increase the grill Smoke Temperature too high and preheat the lid closed for 10 minutes.

8. Place hoagie buns cut side up on a small sheet tray. Fill with the shredded roast and top with a slice of cheese. Transfer to the grill and cook for another 5-10 minutes or until the cheese is melted.

9. Remove from the grill and top with chopped pickled veggies. Serve with remaining cooking liquid for dipping if desired. Enjoy!

Nutrition: Calories: 523g Carbohydrates: 1g | Protein: 55g | Fat: 32g | Saturated Fat: 14g Cholesterol: 195mg | Sodium: 1114mg Potassium: 973mg Vitamin A: 35g Calcium: 52g Iron: 6g

18. *Lamb Wraps*

Preparation Time: 1 hour

Cooking Time: 2 hours

Servings: 4

Ingredients

- 1 leg of lamb
- 3 lemons, juiced
- Olive oil
- Big game rub
- 2 cups yogurt
- 2 cucumbers, diced
- 2 cloves garlic, minced
- 4 tablespoons dill, finely diced
- 2 tablespoons mint leaves, finely diced
- Salt and pepper
- 12 pitas
- 3 tomatoes, diced
- 1 red onion, thinly sliced
- 8 oz. feta cheese

Directions:

1. Rub your lamb with lemon juice, olive oil, and rub.

2. When ready to cook, set your smoker temperature to 500°F and preheat. Put the leg of lamb on the smoker and cook for 30 minutes.

3. Lower the heat to 350 deg and keep cooking for another hour.

4. While the lamb is roasting, create the tzatziki sauce by mixing the yogurt, cucumbers, garlic, dill, mint leaves, in a bowl and mix to combine. Place in the refrigerator to chill.

5. Get the pittas and wrap them in foil, then place them on the grill to warm.

6. Place the lamb on a cutting board and leave to rest for 15 minutes before slicing.

7. Fill the warm pita with red onion, lamb, diced tomato, tzatziki sauce, and feta.

Nutrition: Calories 390, Total fat 35g, Saturated fat 15g, Total Carbs 0g, Net Carbs 0g, Protein 17g, Sugar 0g, Fiber 0g, Sodium: 65mg.

19. Morrocan Kebabs

Preparation Time: 20 minutes

Cooking Time: 30 minutes

Servings: 2

Ingredients

- 1 cup onions, finely diced
- 1 tablespoon fresh mint, finely diced
- 1 teaspoon paprika
- 1 teaspoon salt
- 1/2 teaspoon ground coriander
- 1/4 teaspoon ground cinnamon
- Pita Bread
- 2 cloves garlic, minced
- 3 tablespoons cilantro leaves, finely diced
- 1 tablespoon ground cumin
- 1 1/2 lbs. ground lamb

Directions:

1. In a bowl, mix the ingredients except for the pita bread. Mix into meatballs, and skewer each meatball.

2. Next, wet your hands with water and shape the meat into a sausage shape about as large as your thumb. Cover and refrigerate for 30 minutes.

3. When ready to cook, set your smoker temperature to 350°F and preheat. Put the kebabs on the smoker and cook for 30 minutes.

4. Serve with the pita bread.

Nutrition: Calories 390, Total fat 35g, Saturated fat 15g, Total Carbs 0g, Net Carbs 0g, Protein 17g, Sugar 0g, Fiber 0g, Sodium: 65mg.

20. Steamed Lamb Shank

Preparation Time: 15 minutes

Cooking Time: 4 hours

Servings: 4

Ingredients

- 4 lamb shanks
- Prime rib rub
- 1 cup beef broth
- 1 cup red wine
- 4 sprigs of rosemary and thyme

Directions:

1. Season the lamb with the prime rib rub.
2. Turn your smoker to 500 deg and preheat.
3. Place the lamb straight on the grill and smoke for 20 minutes.
4. Transfer the lamb to a pan and pour in the wine, beef broth, and herbs. Cover and put back on the grill, lowering the temperature to 325 deg.
5. Braise the lamb for 4 hours before serving.

Nutrition: Calories 390, Total fat 35g, Saturated fat 15g, Total Carbs 0g, Net Carbs 0g, Protein 17g, Sugar 0g, Fiber 0g, Sodium: 65mg.

21. Braised Lamb Tacos

Preparation Time: Two Hours

Cooking Time: Five hours

Servings: 4

Ingredients

- 1/4 tablespoon cumin seeds
- 1/4 tablespoon coriander seeds
- 1/4 tablespoon pumpkin seeds
- 2 oz. guajillo peppers
- 1 tablespoon paprika
- 1 tablespoon lime juice
- 1 tablespoon fresh oregano, diced
- 3 cloves garlic, minced
- 2 tablespoons olive oil
- 1 tablespoon salt
- 3 lbs. lamb shoulders

Directions:

1. Grind all of the seeds together before microwaving the chilis with water for two minutes on high.

2. Mix the seeds, lime juice, paprika, garlic cloves, salt, oil, and oregano with the chilis.

3. Place the lamb in a roasting pan, and rub the seasoning mixture over it. Leave for two hours in the fridge.

4. When ready to cook, turn your smoker to 325 deg and preheat.

5. Add 1/2 cup of water to the pan and cover with foil. Cook the lamb for two hours, adding water when needed.

6. Discard the foil and cook for 2 hours more, then leave for 20 minutes before shredding.

7. Serve on corn tortillas.

Nutrition: Calories 390, Total fat 35g, Saturated fat 15g, Total Carbs 0g, Net Carbs 0g, Protein 17g, Sugar 0g, Fiber 0g, Sodium: 65mg.

PORK RECIPES

22. *Simple Wood Pellet Smoked Pork Ribs*

Preparation Time: 15 Minutes

Cooking Time: 5 Hours

Servings: 7

Ingredients:

- Three rack baby back ribs
- 3/4 cup pork and poultry rub
- 3/4 cup Que BBQ Sauce

Directions:

1. Peel the membrane from the backside of the ribs and trim any fat.
2. Season the pork generously with the rub.
3. Set the wood pellet grill to 180°F and preheat for 15 minutes with the lid closed.
4. Place the pork ribs on the grill and smoke them for 5 hours.
5. Remove it from the grill and wrap them in a foil with the BBQ sauce.
6. Place back the pork and increase the temperature to 350°F— Cook for 45 more minutes.

7. Remove the pork from the grill and let it rest for 20 minutes before serving. Enjoy.

Nutrition: Calories 762 Total Fat 57g Saturated Fat 17g Total Carbs 23g Net Carbs 22.7g Protein 39g Sugar 18g Fiber 0.5g Sodium: 737mg Potassium 618mg

23. Roasted Pork with Balsamic Strawberry Sauce

Preparation Time: 15 Minutes

Cooking Time: 35 Minutes

Servings: 3

Ingredients:

- 2 lb. pork tenderloin
- Salt and pepper to taste
- 2 tbsp rosemary, dried
- 2 tbsp olive oil
- 12 strawberries, fresh
- 1 cup balsamic vinegar
- 4 tbsp sugar

Directions:

1. Set the wood pellet grill to 350°F and preheat for 15 minutes with a closed lid.
2. Meanwhile, rinse the pork and pat it dry—season with salt, pepper, and rosemary.
3. In an oven skillet, heat oil until smoking. Add the pork and sear on all sides until golden brown.
4. Set the skillet in the grill and cook for 20 minutes or until the meat is no longer pink and the internal temperature is 150°F.
5. Remove the pork from the grill and let rest for 10 minutes.

6. Add berries to the skillet and sear over the stovetop for a minute. Remove the strawberries from the skillet.

7. Add vinegar in the same skillet and scrape any browned bits from the skillet bottom. Bring it to a boil, then reduce heat to low. Stir in sugar and cook until it has reduced by half.

8. Slice the meat and place the strawberries on top, then drizzle vinegar sauce. Enjoy.

Nutrition: Calories 244 Total Fat 9g Saturated Fat 3g Total Carbs 15g Net Carbs 13g Protein 25g Sugar 12g Fiber 2g Sodium: 159mg

24. Cocoa Crusted Pork Tenderloin

Preparation Time: 30 Minutes

Cooking Time: 25 Minutes

Servings: 5

Ingredients:

- One pork tenderloin
- 1/2 tbsp fennel, ground
- 2 tbsp cocoa powder, unsweetened
- 1 tbsp smoked paprika
- 1/2 tbsp kosher salt
- 1/2 tbsp black pepper
- 1 tbsp extra virgin olive oil
- Three green onion

Directions:

1. Remove the silver skin and the connective tissues from the pork loin.
2. Combine the rest of the ingredients in a mixing bowl, then rub the mixture on the pork. Refrigerate for 30 minutes.
3. Preheat the wood pellet grill for 15 minutes with the lid closed.

4. Sear all sides of the loin at the front of the grill, then reduce the temperature to 350°F and move the pork to the center grill.

5. Cook for 15 more minutes or until the internal temperature is 145°F.

6. Remove from grill and let rest for 10 minutes before slicing. Enjoy

Nutrition: Calories 264 Total fat 13.1g Saturated fat 6g Total Carbs 4.6g Net Carbs 1.2g Protein 33g Sugar 0g Fiber 3.4g Sodium: 66mg

25. Wood Pellet Grilled Bacon

Preparation Time: 30 Minutes

Cooking Time: 25 Minutes

Servings: 6

Ingredients:

- 1 lb. bacon, thickly cut

Directions:

1. Preheat your wood pellet grill to 375°F.
2. Line a baking sheet with parchment paper, then place the bacon on it in a single layer.
3. Close the lid and bake for 20 minutes. Flip over, close the top, and bake for an additional 5 minutes.
4. Serve with the favorite side and enjoy it.

Nutrition: Calories 315 Total fat 14g Saturated fat 10g Protein 9g Sodium: 500mg

APPETIZERS AND SIDES

26. *Cheesy Sausage Balls*

Preparation Time: 15 minutes

Cooking Time: 30 minutes

Servings 4 to 5

Ingredients:

- 1 pound (454 g) ground hot sausage, uncooked
- 8 ounces (227 g) cream cheese, softened
- 1 package mini filo dough shells

Directions:

1. Supply your smoker with wood pellets and follow the manufacturer's specific start-up procedure. Preheat, with the lid closed, to 350°F (177°C).
2. In a large bowl, using your hands, thoroughly mix the sausage and cream cheese until well blended.
3. Place the filo dough shells on a rimmed perforated pizza pan or into a mini muffin tin.
4. Roll the sausage and cheese mixture into 1-inch balls and place into the filo shells.

5. Place the pizza pan or mini muffin tin on the grill, close the lid and smoke the sausage balls for 30 minutes, or until cooked through and the sausage is no longer pink.

6. Plate and serve warm.

Nutrition: Calories: 57 Total Fat: 3 g Saturated Fat: 1 g Total Carbs: 6 g Net Carbs: 4 g Protein: 4 g Sugars: 2 g Fiber: 2 g Sodium: 484 mg

27. Corn and Crab Cakes

Preparation Time: 25 minutes

Cooking Time: 10 minutes

Servings 30 mini crab cakes

Ingredients

- Nonstick cooking spray, oil, or butter, for greasing
- 1 cup panko bread crumbs, divided
- 1 cup canned corn, drained
- ½ cup chopped scallions, divided
- ½ red bell pepper, finely chopped
- 16 ounces (454 g) jumbo lump crab meat
- ¾ cup mayonnaise, divided
- 1 egg, beaten
- 1 teaspoon salt
- 1 teaspoon freshly ground black pepper
- 2 teaspoons cayenne pepper, divided
- Juice of 1 lemon

Directions:

1. Supply your smoker with wood pellets and follow the manufacturer's specific start-up procedure. Preheat, with the lid closed, to 425°F (218°C).

2. Spray three 12-cup mini muffin pans with cooking spray and divide ½ cup of the panko between 30 of the muffin cups, pressing into the bottoms and up the sides. (Work in batches, if necessary, depending on the number of pans you have.)

3. In a medium bowl, combine the corn, ¼ cup of scallions, bell pepper, crab meat, half of the mayonnaise, the egg, salt, pepper, and 1 teaspoon of cayenne pepper.

4. Gently fold in the remaining ½ cup of bread crumbs and divide the mixture between the prepared mini muffin cups.

5. Place the pans on the grill grate, close the lid, and smoke for 10 minutes, or until golden brown.

6. In a small bowl, combine the lemon juice and the remaining mayonnaise, scallions, and cayenne pepper to make a sauce.

7. Brush the tops of the mini crab cakes with the sauce and serve hot.

Nutrition: Calories: 57 Total Fat: 3 g Saturated Fat: 1 g Total Carbs: 6 g Net Carbs: 4 g Protein: 4 g Sugars: 2 g Fiber: 2 g Sodium: 484 mg

28. *Brisket Baked Beans*

Preparation Time:20 Min

Cooking Time:90 Min – 120 Min

Servings:10

Ingredients:

- 1 green bell pepper (medium, diced)
- 1 red bell pepper (medium, diced)
- 1 yellow onion (large, diced)
- 2 - 6 jalapeno peppers (diced)
- 1 can be baked
- 2 tablespoons olive oil (extra-virgin)
- 3 cups brisket flat (chopped)
- beans (28 ounces)
- 1 can red kidney beans (1 4ounces, rinsed, drained)
- 1 cup barbecue sauce
- ½ cup brown sugar (packed)
- 2 teaspoons mustard (ground)
- 3 cloves of garlic (chopped)
- 1 ½ teaspoon black pepper
- 1 ½ teaspoon kosher salt

Directions:

1. Put a skillet on the fire, on medium heat. Warm-up your olive oil. Toss in the diced jalapenos, peppers, and onions. Stir now and then for 8 minutes.

2. Grab a 4-quart casserole dish. Now, in your dish, mix in the pork and beans, kidney beans, baked beans, chopped brisket, cooked peppers and onions, brown sugar, barbecue sauce, garlic, mustard, salt, and black pepper.

3. Set up your wood pellet smoker grill so it's ready for indirect cooking.

4. Preheat your grill to 325°F, using whatever pellets you want.

5. Cook your brisket beans on the grill, for 90 minutes to 120 minutes. Keep it uncovered as you cook. When it's ready, you'll know, because the beans will get thicker and will have bubbles as well.

6. Rest the food for 15 minutes, before you finally move on to step number 5.

7. Serve!

Nutrition: Calories: 200 Fat: 2g Cholesterol: 10mg Carbs: 35g Protein: 9g Intolerances: Gluten-Free, Egg-Free, Lactose-Free

29. Twice-Baked Spaghetti Squash

Preparation Time:15 Min

Cooking Time:45 Min

Servings:2

Ingredients:

- 1 spaghetti squash (medium)
- 1 tablespoon olive oil (extra virgin)
- 1 teaspoon salt
- ½ teaspoon pepper
- ½ cup Parmesan cheese (grated,
- divided)
- ½ cup mozzarella cheese (shredded, divided)

Directions:

1. Cut the squash along the length in half. Make sure you're using a knife that's large enough, and sharp enough. Once you're done, take out the pulp and the seeds from each half with a spoon.
2. Rub the insides of each half of the squash with some olive oil. When you're done with that, sprinkle the salt and pepper.
3. Set up your wood pellet smoker grill for indirect cooking.
4. Preheat your grill to 375°F with your preferred wood pellets.

5. Put each half of the squash on the grill. Make sure they're both facing upwards on the grill grates, which should be nice and hot.

6. Bake for 45 minutes, keeping it on the grill until the internal temperature of the squash hits 170°F. You'll know you're done when you find it easy to pierce the squash with a fork.

7. Move the squash to your cutting board. Let it sit there for 10 minutes, so it can cool a bit.

8. Turn up the temp on your wood pellet smoker grill to 425°F.

9. Use a fork to remove the flesh from the squash in strands by raking it back and forth. Do be careful, because you want the shells to remain intact. The strands you rake off should look like spaghetti if you're doing it right.

10. Put the spaghetti squash strands in a large bowl, and then add in half of your mozzarella and half of your Parmesan cheeses. Combine them by stirring.

11. Take the mix, and stuff it into the squash shells. When you're done, sprinkle them with the rest of the Parmesan and mozzarella cheeses.

12. Optional: You can top these with some bacon bits if you like.

13. Allow the stuffed spaghetti squash shells you've now stuffed to bake at 435°F for 15 minutes, or however long it takes the cheese to go brown.

14. Serve and enjoy.

Nutrition: Calories 214 Fat: 3g Cholesterol: 17mg Carbs: 27g Protein: 16g Intolerances: Egg-Free

30. Bacon-Wrapped Asparagus

Preparation Time:15 MIN

Cooking Time:25 – 30 MIN

Servings:6

Ingredients:

- 15 - 20 spears of fresh asparagus (1 pound)
- Olive oil (extra virgin)
- 5 slices bacon (thinly sliced)
- 1 teaspoon salt and pepper (or your preferred rub)

Directions:

1. Break off the ends of the asparagus, then trim it all so they're down to the same length.
2. Separate the asparagus into bundles—3 spears per bundle. Then spritz them with some olive oil.
3. Use a piece of bacon to wrap up each bundle. When you're done, lightly dust the wrapped bundle with some salt and pepper to taste or your preferred rub.
4. Set up your wood pellet smoker grill so that it's ready for indirect cooking.
5. Put some fiberglass mats on your grates. Make sure they're the fiberglass kind. This will keep your asparagus from getting stuck on your grill gates.

6. Preheat your grill to 400°F, with whatever pellets you prefer. You can do this as you prep your asparagus.

7. Grill the wraps for 25 minutes to 30 minutes, tops. The goal is to get your asparagus looking nice and tender, and the bacon deliciously crispy.

Nutrition: Calories: 71 Fat: 3g Carbs: 1g Protein: 6g Intolerances: Gluten-Free, Egg-Free, Lactose-Free

VEGETARIAN RECIPES

31. *Smoked Cauliflower*

Preparation Time: 15 minutes

Cooking Time: 20-30 minutes

Servings: 4

Ingredients:

- 1 head of cauliflower (separated into florets)
- 2 tbsp cilantro (fresh and minced)
- 2tbsp extra virgin olive oil
- 2 tsp lemon juice
- 1 tsp curry powder
- 2 tsp garlic powder
- 1/4 tsp freshly grounded pepper
- 1/2 tsp salt
- 2 tsp curry powder

Directions:

1. Preheat the Electric Smoker at 2750F. In a large bowl, add 1 tbsp olive oil, salt, pepper, garlic powder, curry, cauliflower, and mix well to coat. Spread evenly on the cooking grates of the electric smoker.

2. Smoke for 20-30 minutes; while smoking, mix 1 tbsp of oil and lemon juice in a bowl. Remove the Cauliflower and drizzle with the lemon mixture. Garnish with cilantro.

Nutrition: Calories: 70 Carbs: 12g Fat: 3g Protein: 13

32. Smoked Cheesy Potatoes Casserole

Preparation Time: 15 minutes

Cooking Time: 60-90 minutes

Servings: 8

Ingredients:

- 1 bag of potatoes (shredded)
- 2 cups sour cream
- 1 cups of chopped onions
- 1/2 cup butter (melted)
- 1 can chicken soup
- 2 cup of cheddar cheese (shredded)
- 1/2 tsp garlic powder
- 1/2 tsp salt
- 1/2 tsp grounded pepper

Directions:

1. Preheat the Electric Smoker to 250F. Mix all the fixings until they are well blended in a large bowl.
2. Pour into a baking pan, then transfer to the cooking grates of the smoker. Smoke for 60-90 minutes or until the top of the casserole turns golden. Serve hot.

Nutrition: Calories: 370 Carbs: 48g Fat: 43g Protein: 30g

33. Vegetarian Hot Dogs with Spicy Jalapeño Relish

Preparation Time: 10 Minutes

Cooking Time: 12 to 14 Minutes

Servings: 5

Ingredients:

- 8 hot dog-size carrots, peeled
- ¼ cup honey
- ¼ cup yellow mustard
- Nonstick cooking spray or butter, for greasing
- Salt
- Freshly ground black pepper
- 8 hot dog buns
- Sweet and Spicy Jalapeño Relish

Directions:

1. Prepare the carrots by removing the stems and slicing in half lengthwise.
2. In a small bowl, whisk together the honey and mustard.
3. Supply your smoker with wood pellets and follow the manufacturer's specific start-up procedure. Preheat, with the lid, closed, to 375 degrees F.

4. Line a baking sheet with aluminum foil and coat with cooking spray.

5. Brush the carrots on both sides with the honey mustard and season with salt and pepper; put on the baking sheet.

6. Place the baking sheet on the grill grate, close the lid, and smoke for 35 to 40 minutes, or until tender and starting to brown.

7. To serve, lightly toast the hot dog buns on the grill and top each with two slices of carrot and some relish.

Smoking Tip: Be sure to fully preheat your smoker to the temperature called for before placing carrots (or any roasting vegetables) on the grill.

Nutrition: Amount per 210 g = 1 serving(s) Calories: 150 Carbohydrates: 15 g Protein: 79 g Sodium: 45 Cholesterol: 49 mg

34. *Grilled Citrus Shrimp Lettuce Cups*

Preparation Time: 30 minutes

Cooking Time: 5 minutes

Servings: 8

Ingredients:

- 1 small finely chopped shallot
- 1 5inch lemongrass stalk, outer layers removed and finely chopped
- 1 thinly sliced Thai chili
- ½ cup fresh lime juice
- ½ cup fresh orange juice
- 2 tsp. of finely chopped peeled ginger
- 1 tsp. (or more) Kosher salt
- 1 pound of peeled, deveined large shrimp, tails removed
- 2 tsp. of toasted sesame oil cooked white rice, Little Gem lettuce leaves, sliced cucumber or julienned carrot, lime wedges, mint sprigs, and toasted sesame seeds

Directions:

1. Mix the shallot, lemongrass, chili, lime and orange juice, ginger, and salt in a little bowl. Cover and let it take a seat at room temperature. Pour some marinade over the shrimp in a medium bowl, cowl, and relax for 30 mins. Set up the grill for

medium-excessive heat. Grill the shrimp till softly sang and cooked through, approximately 1–2 minutes for each facet. Move the shrimp right into a big bowl and blend with sesame oil, then season with salt.

2. Serve the shrimp with rice, lettuce, cucumber or carrots, lime wedges, mint, sesame seeds, and marinade for making lettuce cups.

Nutrition: Amount per 202 g = 1 serving(s) Energy (calories): 308 kcal Protein: 13.46 g Fat: 20.52 g Carbohydrates: 18.19 g

35. *Broccoli and Cheddar Stuffed Potatoes*

Preparation Time: 15 minutes

Cooking Time: 1 hour & 25 minutes

Servings: 10

Ingredients:

- 1 oz russet tomatoes
- 2 cups of broccoli florets (cut to 1-inch thick)
- 1 tsp freshly chopped chives
- 1/2 cup sour cream
- 1 cup of bacon (chopped)
- 2 cups of cheddar cheese (shredded)
- 1/4 tsp salt
- 1/4 tsp pepper

Directions:

1. Preheat the Electric Smoker to 275F. Using a fork, make incisions all over the potatoes. Arrange on the cooking grates and smoke for 45 minutes or until it can be pierced easily with a fork.

2. Remove from the oven and allow to cool. Reduce the temperature of the Electric Smoker to 250F. Cut the potatoes into lengthwise halves and scoop out the insides to within 1/8 inch into a bowl.

3. Add cheddar cheese, bacon, sour cream, broccoli, salt, pepper, and mash together. Spoon in the potato mixture back into the potato shells, top with cheddar cheese.

4. Arrange on the grates and smoke for another 30-40 minutes or until the cheese has melted. Sprinkle with chives and serve.

Nutrition: Calories: 197 Carbs: 32g Fat: 3g Protein: 11g

36. *Aromatic Smoked Duck Breast*

Preparation Time: 15 minutes + marinate time

Cooking Time: 3 hours 10 minutes

Servings: 5

Preferred Wood Pellet: Cherry

Ingredients:

- 3 pounds duck breast
- For Marinade:
- 3 cups apple juice
- 1 tbsp. salt
- 1 and ½ tbsp. sugar
- 2 tbsp. soy sauce
- ¾ tsp. paprika
- ¾ tsp. garlic powder
- 1 tsp. dried basils
- ¾ tsp. pepper

Directions:

1. Add apple juice into a container and season with salt, sugar, soy sauce, paprika, garlic powder, dried basil, pepper, and stir well

2. Score duck breast at several places and put breast into the marinade, marinate for 4 hours

3. Pre-heat your smoker to 325 degrees F, remove the breast from marinade and place it in the smoker

4. Smoke until the internal temperature reaches 325 degrees F

5. Remove and cut smoked duck breast into thick slices, serve and enjoy!

Nutrition: Amount per 201 g = 1 serving(s) Energy (calories): 136 kcal Protein: 7.48 g Fat: 2.82 g

Carbohydrates: 20.42 g

37. Smoked Quails

Preparation Time: 15minutes + marinate time

Cook Time: 1 hour 10 minutes

Servings: 4

Preferred Wood Pellet: Alder

Ingredients:

- 5 pounds quails
- For Marinade:
- 2 cups orange juice
- 1 cup of soy sauce
- 2 tbsp. garlic, minced
- ½ cup brown sugar
- ¼ cup olive oil
- 1 tbsp. pepper
- 1 cup onion, chopped

Directions:

1. Add orange juice into a container and add soy sauce, garlic, brown sugar, olive oil, pepper, onion, and stir well
2. Add quails to container and toss well to coat
3. Cover the container with id and marinate quail for 3 hours
4. Marinate quails overnight
5. Pre-heat your Smoker to 225 degrees F

6. Add quails (breast side up) and smoke for 1 hour until internal temperature reaches 145 degrees F

7. Once done, remove and serve

8. Enjoy!

Nutrition: Amount per 283 g = 1 serving(s) Energy (calories): 417 kcal Protein: 43.2 g Fat: 16.98 g

Carbohydrates: 20.78 g

38. Smoked Venison

Preparation Time: 10 minutes

Cooking Time: 2 hours

Servings: 4

Ingredients:

- 1 lb. of venison tenderloin
- ¼ cup of lemon juice
- ¼ cup of olive oil
- 5 minced garlic cloves
- 1 tsp. of salt
- 1 tsp. of ground black pepper

Directions:

1. Start by putting the whole venison tenderloin in a zip-style bag or a large bowl.
2. Add the lemon juice, olive oil, garlic, salt, and pepper into a food processor
3. Process your ingredients until they are very well incorporated
4. Pour the marinade on top of the venison; then massage it in very well
5. Refrigerate and let marinate for about 4 hours or an overnight

6. When you are ready to cook, just remove your marinade's venison and rinse it off very well.

7. Pat the meat dry and let it come to room temperature for about 30 minutes before cooking it

8. In the meantime, preheat your smoker to a temperature of about 225°F

9. Smoke the tenderloin for about 2 hours

10. Let the meat rest for about 10 minutes before slicing it

11. Top with black pepper; then serve and enjoy your dish!

Nutrition: Amount per 159 g = 1 serving(s) Energy (calories): 302 kcal Protein: 34.42 g Fat: 16.24 g

Carbohydrates: 3.36 g

39. *Smoked Rabbit*

Preparation Time: 15 minutes + 60 minutes marinate time

Cooking Time: 2 hours

Servings: 5

Preferred Wood Pellet: Alder

Ingredients:

- 1 cottontail skinned and gutted
- 2 tbsp. salt
- ½ cup white vinegar
- Water as needed
- For Rub:
- 1 tbsp. garlic powder
- 1 tbsp. cayenne pepper
- 1 tbsp. salt
- 1 bottle BBQ sauce

Directions:

1. Take a bowl and add in your kosher salt alongside the white vinegar to make your brine
2. Pour the brine over your rabbit using a shallow dish and add just enough water to cover up the whole of your rabbit
3. Let it sit for an hour
4. Pre-heat your smoker to a temperature of 200 degrees F.

5. Take a bowl and whisk in the garlic powder, salt, pepper, and cayenne pepper to make the rubbing

6. Season the rabbit nicely

7. Toss your rabbit in your smoker and add the hickory wood to your wood chamber

8. Let it smoke for two hours and keep adding wood pellets after every 15 minutes

9. Remove the rabbit from your smoker and serve hot

Nutrition: Amount per 138 g = 1 serving(s) Energy (calories): 93 kcal Protein: 3.31 g Fat: 0.3 g Carbohydrates: 19.44 g

40. *Spiced Nuts*

Preparation Time: 5 minutes

Cooking Time: 20 minutes

Servings: 32 tablespoons

Ingredients:

- 1 teaspoon dried rosemary
- 1/8 teaspoon cayenne pepper
- 1/8 teaspoon ground black pepper
- ½ teaspoon salt or to taste
- ½ teaspoon ground cumin
- 1 tablespoon olive oil
- 2 tablespoon maple syrup
- 2/3 cup raw and unsalted cashew nuts
- 2/3 cup raw and unsalted pecans
- 2/3 cup raw and unsalted walnuts

Directions:

1. Start your grill on smoke mode, leaving the lid open for 5 minutes, until the fire starts.

2. Close the grill lid and preheat the grill to 350°F.

3. In a large bowl, combine all the ingredients except the dried rosemary. Mix thoroughly until the ingredients are evenly mixed, and all nuts are coated with spices.

4. Spread the spiced nuts on a baking sheet.

5. Place the baking sheet on the grill and roast the nuts for 20 to 25 minutes.

6. Remove the nuts from heat.

7. Sprinkle the dried rosemary on the nuts and stir to mix.

8. Leave the nuts to cool for a few minutes.

9. Serve and enjoy.

Nutrition: Calories: 64 | Total Fat: 5.8g | Saturated Fat: 0.4g Cholesterol: 0mg | Sodium: 35mg

Total Carbohydrate: 2.2g Dietary Fiber: 0.6g Total Sugars: 0.8g | Protein: 1.3g

CPSIA information can be obtained
at www.ICGtesting.com
Printed in the USA
BVHW091919240621
610370BV00002B/102